Life, Death and everything in between

Michelle Leonard

Presentation by *BookLeaf Publishing*

Web: www.bookleafpub.com

E-mail: info@bookleafpub.com

ISBN: 9789357613347

First edition 2022

I couldn't have written this without my family, especially my parents Sharon and David, my partner Eddie and my children Caolan, Kiara and Cain. I love you all

ACKNOWLEDGEMENT

A massive thanks to Bookleaf Publishing for giving me this opportunity to finally get published, and to everyone who encouraged me along the way. Special thanks goes to Kirsty Callaly who gave me the kick I needed to get up and get things moving!!

Death

I felt the freezing hand of Death
Graze my forehead while I slept
I stretched out and I gave a yawn
When my eyes opened, Death was gone

I think that I saw Death today
While I watched my children play
But when I got up and walked near
The ghostly figure disappeared

I know that I heard Death tonight
I looked, but he was out of sight
I shivered as he called my name
And watched my husband do the same

I tasted Death today, it's true
I swear I wouldn't lie to you
He stood aside and watched me bake
His flavour entered every cake

I smelt Death today, that was hard
I was instantly on my guard
He's coming close, it's plain to see
Quite soon he'll reach his target...me

I went out in my car today
I went to my local church to pray
I didn't see him standing there
Though he didn't hide, he didn't care

I started driving home and saw
A little boy chasing a ball
I glimpsed his mother's anguished face
As I screamed out and hit the brakes

I swerved to the other side of the road
Then looked up and my blood ran cold
In my panic I'd failed to heed
The truck approaching at great speed

I heard a crash but felt no pain
As my body was flung out in the rain
I saw a shadow and closed my eyes
Here came Death to claim his prize

I knew then that my time had come
I didn't hurt, I just felt numb
I closed my eyes and began to cry
Asked why he'd chosen me to die

I sensed a coldness coming near
He harshly whispered in my ear
"Don't worry, this won't hurt at all
For you saved that child chasing his ball"

I suddenly saw I was wearing white
As Death drew me towards a blinding light
"You were loved" he said, "very much so
But now I'm afraid it's time to go"

I took his hand but paused a while
Looked back at my body and gave a smile
My family would grieve, but I knew this was
right
I walked forward with Death, and entered the
light

Life's Too Short

Stop and smell the roses
I've often heard it said
Life's too short to have these
Types of thoughts in your head

Life's too short to panic
Life's too short to cry
Life's too short to worry
Life's precious, till you die

You may not think you're worth much
You may think you're a mess
But life's too short to think like this
Life's short, just be your best

Life's too short to wonder
What else you could have done
You've started on your journey
Remember you're number one

Life's too short to waste it
On crying, no more tears!!
Life's too short to deal with
These different types of fears

Lifes too short for anything
But still you feel a pull
So stop and smell those roses
And live life to the full

To My Family

I have something I want to tell you
On a subject that's close to my heart
I've tried before so many times
But I didn't know where to start

You think you know all about me
You see my happy smiling face
But you don't see the darkness
That comes to take its place

I know that today I seem happy
I'm showing my cheerful side
But I feel it's time to tell you
About the "me" I've been trying to hide

You see, I have a mental illness
That's a major part of me
And I feel it can take over
The person I used to be

People ask me out for drinks
And I don't know how to say
That this monster deep inside me
Is best kept well at bay

When I wake up in the morning
Feeling useless and no good
It's my mental illness at work
It's putting me in this mood

I'll smile, I'll joke, I'll laugh, I'll play
I'll show the world my mask
And if I let my false face slip
Nobody wants to ask

I'm still a lovely person
I'm still the same old me
But here's the situation
That I need you to see

I find it hard to explain
I don't expect you to understand
But all I ask from you is
A little helping hand

Know that when I'm grumpy
It's nothing that you've said
It's just that awful feeling
Deep inside my head

It can try to take me over
But I'll always push it back
I won't let it drag me
Into that pool of black

So if sometimes you see me
And I'm not feeling too well
I just need an opportunity
To get out of my hell

A smile, a touch, a simple word
A cuddle or a kiss
These are what I need from you
So can you promise this?

Whenever this damned illness
Comes rushing to the fore
Give me your understanding
I could ask for nothing more

I love you all so dearly
You're my world, my life, my light
And I know with your support
I'll never give up this fight

Mama

I'm right here with you mama
I'm with you every day
I just can't wait to see you
To grow and learn to play

I always hear you talking
Your voice makes me feel safe
I'll be with you soon mama
Soon I'll see your face

But somethings happened mama
I heard my daddy shout
He doesn't want a baby
What's he talking about?

He can't mean I'm the baby
Doesn't he want me there?
Mama give me comfort
Please mama, I'm so scared

We went walking today mama
I heard you with your friends
You told them that the day I'm born
Is the day your marriage ends

I just don't understand it
My hearts begun to beat
What's those little things down there?
I think you call them feet?

I'm sucking on my fingers
I'm playing with my toes
Mama I can't wait to meet you
My love for you just grows

I know that daddys angry
But just wait then he'll see
The day I come into the world
I'll bring my love with me

He'll teach me to play football
You'll teach me how to cook
And every night we'll cuddle up
Together with a book

I'm so excited Mama
That day will be here soon
I'm always getting bigger
I'm running out of room!

Mama what's going on out there?
You seem so very sad
Have I done something wrong mama?
Have I somehow been bad?

I hear someone talking mama
They say you need to rest
What do you mean mama
When you say it's for the best?

I can feel you lying down now
But something isn't right
I'm scared mama, please help me
Somethings holding me tight

Mama please, it hurts me
They're taking me from you
Mama now I'm crying
I don't know what to do

I'll never see the sun mama
Or hear your loving voice
I know you would have loved me
But now you don't have that choice

I'm getting weaker mama
It's time to say goodbye
I never knew real life
But I know I don't want to die

I still forgive you mama
You and daddy too
And if you ever think of me
Remember I love you

Kids Are Hard

Kids are hard, kids are mean
Kids are cruel and quite obscene
When they reach the teenage stage
Their attitude changes with age

They can yell and they can fight
They can rebel with all their might
They can say that hate your guts
They can drive you completely nuts

But beyond that hormonal part
Deep inside their childish heart
They love you really, yes they do
There's no-one who compares to you

So take a breath and count to ten
Calm yourself, breathe out and then
Remember they're young women or men
So take a breath and count again!!

Survivor

I gave you my heart
I gave you my soul
I dropped my defences
I gave you my whole

I told you my hopes
I told you my fears
I told you what things
Could reduce me to tears

I shared all my secrets
I shared all my dreams
But I just didn't know
That you weren't what you seemed

I opened my home
I opened my life
You told me that one day
You'd make me your wife

I thought I was happy
I thought you were true
I thought that I'd never
Find a good man like you

We made lifetime plans
We'd travel the world
But all of a sudden
My dreams just unfurled

You tried to inform me
What way I should dress
I did as you wanted
I avoided stress

I wanted to go out
With my friends at night
But when I got ready
You called me a fright

I was making movies
And having a ball
Even when I was busy
I'd come when you'd call

I neglected my family
I neglected my son
At this stage in my life
You were my only one

I'd have walked over lava
If it would make you smile
I was under your spell
For too long of a while

I just didn't realize
I was under your spell
Every time you yelled at me
I was going through hell

I did all I could for you
Nowhere else left to turn
The longer we were together
Those hell fires burned

You had never beaten me
Never hurt me that way
When I heard the word "abuse"
I just waved it away

It took me such a long time
To see what was wrong
I didn't quite realize
Until you were gone

Domestic violence
Works in more ways than one
You don't need to hit people
Or hurt them "in fun"

You abused me badly
You destroyed my trust
I may never get better

But this is a must

I'm back with ny family
I'm back with my son
I'm remembering how
I used to have fun

I'll always remember
What you did to me
But my eyes have been opened
And now I can see

I thought I was a victim
Of domestic abuse
Couldn't do anything right
Was never any use

But now I can see
That I'm much better now
It'll be a long journey
But right here is my vow

I'll keep on fighting
Each and every day
I'm a goddamned survivor
And I'm finding my way

You'll Be Sorry

You dropped me when I needed you most...
You'll be sorry

You dropped me quickly, left me to coast...
You'll be sorry

I know that certain rules are key...
You'll be sorry

But when I explained you didn't listen to me...
You'll be sorry

I came to you for support and care...
You'll be sorry

But when I asked you were never there...
You'll be sorry

There's a million other people like you...
You'll be sorry

You're nothing special, you're nothing new...
You'll be sorry

Sometime in the future you'll finally learn...

You'll be sorry

I'm sorry but you may just crash and burn...
You'll be sorry

And I'll be watching with my friends way up
high...
You'll be sorry

Kissing my hand and waving goodbye...
You'll be sorry

I Love You

I really can't describe it
This feeling in my heart
I want to talk about these feelings
But I don't know where to start

Every time you look my way
Your love for me shines through
I've never fallen for anyone
The way I fell for you

I want to spend my time with you
Every second of every day
When you wrap your arms around me
That's just where I want to stay

In your embrace is my safe spot
I never want to let you go
I can't tell you what you mean to me
But I think somehow you know

I tingle when you kiss me
I melt at the slightest touch
I hope that this poem shows you
That I love you so so much

The butterflies in my stomach
Seem to be here to stay
But if I'm being honest
I don't want them to go away

For every little flutter
Brings your heart closer to mine
My love for you is endless
With no limits of time

I want to be with you forever
Together we make something great
You're my one, my only
You're my true soulmate

Magic

Do you believe in magic?
I do, and as you'll see
I'm talking about the magic
That surrounds you and me

I don't mean spells and potions
Eye of frog and tail of newt
I don't do things like that
Though it sounds like quite a hoot

I'm speaking of the magic
That surrounds us everywhere
They type that you don't notice
Till someone shows you it's there

Now I'm about to tell you
Just what I mean by this
I'll tell you how this magic
Simply should not be missed

The leaves in the trees change colour
As they fall down to the ground
Little children running through them
It's such a pretty sound

The water flowing gently
In a river or a stream
The sunrise hitting a mountain
Such a memorable scene

A mother bird feeding her babies
As they sit up in their nest
The father flying all day
Then coming back for a rest

The golden warmth of summer
Spreads happiness and cheer
Everybody is smiling
Now the good weathers here

Squirrels hibernate for the cold months
So you can't find them at all
There's Summer and there's Spring
There's Winter and there's Fall

We have nature all around us
Almost everywhere we see
And I don't know about you
But that's magical to me

Last Goodbye

I miss your jokes, I miss your laugh
I miss your perfect smile
I wish that I could have you back
Just for a little while

I miss the way you held me close
Whenever I felt bad
I miss the way you cuddled me
And stopped me being sad

I miss your sense of humour
Your crazy sense of fun
I miss the way you'd tell me
That i was your number one

You'll always be my best friend
The one I'll always love
So this is a poem from my heart
Sent to you up above

You left us far too suddenly
And I can't help but cry
When I think that on that last time
When I couldn't say goodbye

You went on that long journey
From which never can return
Living without you is a hard lesson
But it's one I'll have to learn

Though your Messengers still active
Your Facebooks still going strong
I can no longer write to you
It's starting to feel wrong

I never can forget you
You meant the world to me
But I have to let you go now
I have to leave you be

So here's my final message
Though I think of you all year
And still I can't say your name
Without wiping away a tear

Someday I'll see you again
But not for a long time yet
My work here isn't finished
But I'll never ever forget.

I'll always love you my friend
Now spread your wings and fly
And as for me, still here on Earth
THIS is my last goodbye.

The Voice

I heard a nasty voice today
It told me what to do
Stay away from others
If you know what's good for you.

You're useless and pathetic
Nobody wants you there
It's just you and me kid
Those people? They don't care

They claim they want your company
Always calling your name
You act so strong but deep inside
You're nothing but fair game

You're useless and pathetic
Nobody wants you there
It's just you and me kid
The others? They don't care

The others just aren't like you
They're confident and quick
They'll soon see how slow you are
Your face will make them sick

You're useless and pathetic
Nobody wants you there
It's just you and me kid
Those people? They don't care

But today I made a difference
I shut that voice away
I went to visit others
And I managed to stay

The voice has haunted me for years
Telling me to go
That I should hide away from the world
They just don't want to know

But now I know the difference
People like me for me
I can act just like myself
Not who the voice tells me to be

It's going to be a long journey
I may cry and weep and wail
But this is my promise to myself
I'm not going to fail

I'm not useless or pathetic
People liked to see me there
And today I've finally learnt
That even strangers care

Best Friends

The first time that I met you
At a low point in my life
I knew that we'd be good friends
We'd help each other battle strife

You're so gifted and creative
Always helping others too
Even when you're feeling bad
Your strong side shines right through

You always act happy and bubbly
You make others feel the same
Feeling we have nothing to lose
And everything to gain

That day you walked into my life
Changed my entire mood
You showed me how to live again
How to focus on the good

There aren't many people like you
I hope this poem gives you some clue
Of what our friendship means to me
And how I cherish you

Perfect Imperfection

You think that you're a loser
Not right for anyone
But I'm here to tell you darling
That soon your time will come

You may not see it right now
You want to run away and cry
But venture out and spread your wings
I'm here to help you fly

I know that times can seem dark
You can't see your way through
But I'll tell you what I see
Every time I look at you

I see someone who's clever
Who's funny and who's smart
I see you helping others
I see your gentle heart

I see you when you're not looking
When you're staring into space
With that devastating look
Of loneliness upon your face

I'm always here for company
I'm staying by your side
I'll help you gain confidence again
No need to try to hide

It's time to shine your light now
Show the world who you are
A bright and beautiful person
A perfect shining star

A Mothers Love

I remember the day you were born
The first time I saw your face
You fitted right into my heart
You'd found your special place

I held you gently in my arms
Counted your fingers and toes
I looked into your gorgeous eyes
I kissed your button nose

I remember bringing you home with me
Everything was brand new
But I knew I'd work everything out
As long as I had you

We both grew up together
We taught each other well
What would our futures be like?
I knew that only time would tell

I was there when you took your first steps
When you said your first words
I taught you about nature
About animals and birds

In no time you'd started school
You started to move away from me
I missed you but you were having fun
Your smiles made that plain to see

I watched as you got older
Gradually leaving my side
I remember the day you moved out
I remember how I cried

I stood proudly at your wedding
I managed to smile through my tears
This was the moment you'd waited for
You'd planned this for several years

I remember my first grandchild
You watched your little one with glee
Watching you with your own child
Brought those early days back to me

Yes, we had our good times
We also had our bad
I rejoiced when you were happy
Gave comfort when you were sad

Now you're fully grown
With a family of your own
I miss you every day
But you won't hear me cry or moan

For I've given you a good life
I know that much is true
My life's greatest achievement
Began the day that I met you

Seasons

What's your favourite season?
I think that mines is Spring
It's exploding with new life
The birds again begin to sing

Springtime brings a promise
Of better days ahead
Time to shed those winter clothes
Flowers begin to raise their head

What's your favourite season?
It's summertime for me
I love the hotter weather
People smiling is all I see

Summer holidays are coming
With shorter nights and longer days
Opportunities to have fun
In tons of different ways

What's your favourite season?
Well Autumn would be mine
The leaves change colour and fall down
It's such a beautiful time

The geese all start to migrate
Forming that perfect "V"
Flying off to warmer climates
It's an awesome thing to see

What's your favourite season?
Mines is Winter, it's true
The snow starts gently falling
Making the world seem brand new

With wintertime comes Christmas
Santa, presents and lots of food
I want to stuff my face full
But I'm afraid that would seem rude!

So what's your favourite season?
Is it the same as mine?
We're lucky to live in a world
That changes all the time

Krampus is Coming

Your parents have told me that you have been
bad
And I have to admit that makes me quite mad
Because you refuse to do just what they say
Tonight is the night I can take you away

I'll sneak into your room as you're falling asleep
You won't see or hear me, I won't make a peep
I'll grab you and stuff you deep down in my sack
Say goodbye to your family, you'll never be back

You wouldn't help your family decorate the tree
You've behaved as badly as a kid could possibly
be
You refused to listen to your dad or mum
For that reason, my child, your time has now
come

I'll take you away to that land of my own
With not even a toy to remind you of home
You'll become my slave, your clothes will be
ripped
And if you don't obey me then you shall be
whipped

But there is one way to stop me tonight
Listen to your parents, try to do things right
Just remember from now until Christmas night
Little one, I won't let you out of my sight...

BSL

Have you ever stroked a Pitbull?
Or played football with a Staff?
Have you ever hugged a Rottweiler?
Have they ever made you laugh?

We call them our fur babies
We feed them from our hand
But now just look what's happening
These breeds are getting banned

These dogs get trained for fighting
And as far as I'm aware
They're getting killed because of this
And that just isn't fair

So if you are against this
Then let your voice be heard
Speak up against BSL
And start to spread the word

I wish I'd known you

I was cuddling with Mummy
And she spoke of you today
Of the jokes you used to tell her
And the pranks you used to play

You were a good friend to Mummy
But I never saw your face
I wish that I had met you
And seen your clumsy grace

Today Mummy was crying
She said she missed you so
She never got to say goodbye
Before you had to go

But she talks about you often
And I learn more every day
She shows me all your pictures
And I just want to say

I didn't know you, but I love you
I wish I'd seen your smile
But I know you're looking over me
Still laughing all the while

You're watching us every day
And I hope that you can see
How much you're missed down here
By Mummy and by me

The Intruder

The glass in my front door smashed
As I lay in my bed
Thoughts of an intruder
Started running through my head

What would happen to me
If I ventured down the stairs?
Would my footsteps scare him off?
Would he even care?

I'd sacrifice my jewellery
My money he could take
But he had better not touch
My specially made cake

I'd received this cake yesterday
I hadn't yet taken a bite
My friend was coming over
To help me tomorrow night

I needed help to move house
And she always made things fun
The cake would be our reward
And the end of a job well done

I got out of bed slowly
And crept along the floor
Quickly grabbing the baseball bat
That I kept by the door

I tiptoed down my stairs then
The noises coming near
The man was in the kitchen
At least that much was clear

I held my bat more firmly
My courage almost gone
But the thought of my special cake
Gave me the strength to carry on

I rushed into the kitchen
Quickly turning on the light
There I saw the intruder
That had kept me up all night

He stood there by my counter
Eyes covered by his mask
His hands looked wet and sticky
With what, I didn't like to ask

I saw my half-eaten cake
And I wanted to cry
He'd violated my treat
And for that he'd have to die

Then I stopped and told myself
Not to be such a loon
It turned out my intruder
Was just a damned raccoon!!

Money didn't save me

Some people call me frugal
Some people call me tight
Some people call me cheapskate
You know what? They're all right!

I don't like to spend much
I'll save cash where I can
I'm saving a fortune on rent
By sleeping in my van

£4.99 for a meal deal?
No way, I'll go without
£1 extra for gravy?
Now what's all that about?

People say I have deep pockets
People say I have short arms
People refer to me as Scrooge
But I don't see the harm

It's getting cold now that it's Autumn
I could do with a blanket or two
But I can't bear spending my money
Here's some old papers, they'll do

I'm feeling quite hungry tonight
My value tin of beans is gone
But the takeaways so expensive
I'll just try to sleep till dawn

It hasn't rained here in a fortnight
My throats parched from my thirst
But I won't spend my money on water
I'll drink from a toilet bowl first

I can see a dark shadow above me
The Reaper is coming tonight
I try to call for help but I can't
I pass with my eyes wide with fright

I never spent my money
I saved the best I could
But dying alone in that can
I know now that I probably should

People said I'm parsimonious
If that's words even allowed
But it's true what others have told me
There's no pocket room in a shroud

Jenny

Did you hear about wee Jenny?
A lovely girl, she was
When she walked out through the streets
Every man would pause

Some of these men were single
Others wore wedding rings
Women hated to see her coming
As she was known for casual flings

Take poor old Paul the butcher
Married for forty years
But after one glance from Jenny
His marriage ended in tears

I don't know what it was about her
Was it her looks, her silent grace?
What made these men so adamant
They could live up to her pace?

She tried it with my husband
At least three times this past year
But one withering glance from me
And he knows not to go near

Some women say she charges
Instead of claiming on the dole
Other wives say she's a demon
Who are their husbands soul

"He'd never go for Jenny
She's not his type at all"
I hear those lines so often
It's like their battle call

But I know one thing about her
That could drive her from the town
They say that when crap gets up
It's hard to beat back down

I've known Jenny years now
Should I let her secret slip?
For Jenny was once Jeremy
Until she got the snip!